Before Launching
My First Business

Before Launching My First Business

Raymond Vasquez

To order additional copies of this book, contact:
Xlibris Corporation
1-888-795-4274
www.Xlibris.com
Orders@Xlibris.com
125578

Contents

Business Advice from Someone Who Has Survived Eighteen Years and Counting.

INTRODUCTION

HELLO. MY NAME is Raymond Vasquez a.k.a. Supa Dave. I have been in business, going on my eighteenth year now; it has been a long ride to this point, a very stressful but great, rewarding mission at times. I am writing this book to help all those fresh minds who are thinking about opening a business of their own; I think you should get real advice from someone who has really been in business and has seen all the struggles you can go through.

BUSINESS PLAN

Your business plan

YOUR BUSINESS PLAN should help you identify the cost of equipment, how business makes its profits, and the business expenses and overhead.

Expenses will consist of rent, security deposit, awning or sign, neon lights, location renovation, lights for showcases and displays, central air-conditioning and heating, stock, phone system, credit card machine, register, alarm, insurance, computers, copier machine, fax machine.

Monthly Expenses

1. Rent
2. Electricity
3. Telephone bill
4. Employees
5. Insurance
6. Taxes
7. Alarm system
8. Garbage removal
9. Merchandise or inventory
10. Advertising

TYPE OF LICENSE

License type, business type

Sole proprietorship, partnership, corporation

YOU HAVE TO decide what is best for you: a business under your name with a DBA, doing business as, or a partnership if there's more than one partner again under your names or filling a corporation where you will be better protected under the laws that fall under the umbrella of a corporation. Please get the advice of a lawyer before you proceed.

INSURANCE

YOU NEED TO have insurance to protect your business from fire, water damage, burglary, or someone falling and getting hurt at your establishment. The amount of insurance depends on how much stock and equipment you have and how much it costs to open your business. Please consult with a licensed accountant to be sure you are covered completely.

TAXES

TAXES NEED TO be paid to the government depending on the type of business you open, and you will need to pay weekly, monthly, quarterly, and yearly taxes. Please consult with a licensed accountant to find out what taxes you will be responsible for.

MARKET RESEARCH

MARKET RESEARCH IS your best friend when opening a business, for market research can save you a lot of money and a lot of headaches. I cannot stress to you how important it is for you to do a lot of market research and then some more.

When you do market research, you are trying to answer these questions:

1. Who needs my product and services?
2. Is there another business already offering these services near where I want to open?
3. The demographics in the neighborhood–will the people who live there now need my product or services?
4. The population total–is there enough customers?
5. The rent–will I be able to afford to pay for it?
6. The commute to my business–is there public transportation or highways near my business?
7. Do I speak the language of clients in the neighborhood?
8. Why are customers going to come to me instead of the competition? How will I be different?

LOCATION

Location, Location, Location

Location is crucial to your business being successful.

THE LOCATION IS extremely important because you want to open in a high traffic area but do not have to pay a very high rent from day one; a high rent will get you out of business before six months passes by.

Therefore, you need a nice-sized store in a high traffic area where your rent isn't crazy high.

To be on an avenue, your rent will be $5,000 per month; go to the side street of the avenue and pay $2,000 a month.

LOANS

BUSINESS LOANS ARE very hard to come by. A bank will not lend money to someone who is starting out new business unless they have collateral; just in case the business doesn't work, the bank will keep your properties that you gave them as collateral.

You can borrow from a friend, but he will probably want to charge you interest. You really don't want to add more expenses to your monthly overhead. A loan is only going to add more bills to the bills you have already, and instead of taking that cash to re-up on your stock, you're paying off interest.

Try to open your business with your own cash.

MARKETING
ADVERTISING

YOU WANT TO market your product or services in the immediate area of your business. Don't venture too far and don't spend too much cash at the beginning. The best is word-of-mouth advertising. Be careful not to overspend on the marketing and advertising pace yourself. Advertising can be very expensive. You want to have flyers and business cards or a nice sign in front with a lot of lights.

WHEN IS THE RIGHT TIME?

WHEN IS THE right time to open your business? What season is more relevant to your business? Are you mentally and physically ready to open this business?

The right time is very important as well. You need to be ready both mentally and physically to be capable of running a business. It takes a lot of energy to open and run a business.

EXTRA CASH

I THINK YOU SHOULD have liquid cash at least six months worth of monthly expenses; a year would be ideal, but that's a lot of extra cash to have once you spend a bunch of money to open the business in the first place.

Now, if your overhead is $5,000 bucks a month, six months of that is 30K.

If you can have a nice stash of 30K before you open, you will not be stressed out, and if the business has a slow start, you will be fine because you don't have to scramble to make ends meet.

It takes a while for five businesses to turn a profit, some longer than others. I was scrambling for the first six years of my seventeen years, and every once in a while, I get send a test of endurance, or there is a big drastic change in the marketplace that changes your profit margin.

Having extra liquidated cash is priceless. And will bring you peace of mind.

POSITIONS

THE POSITION AND/OR job description should be well-thought-out before you open. Who will be responsible for opening and closing?

Who will be at the front desk? Who will be responsible to open and close the business? Who will be at back? Who will do the deliveries? All job-related tasks should be given to someone in detail.

The entire process of running the business from A to Z should be written in a book so that there's no confusion as to who has to do what.

LEASE

THE LEASE WILL have the amount of rent you have to pay when it will go up, how much it will go up, and if you have to pay water or taxes.

When negotiating your lease, try to get a few months to renovate for free. Also, try to have your rent fixed for the first three years with no increases. Finally, try to get a long lease–five years, ten years–and make sure that the increase are not more than 2 percent per year.

LEAVING
YOUR CURRENT JOB

I F YOU ARE thinking of leaving your
current job, ask yourself, am I going to
get paid enough from new business venture to continue living the lifestyle I am
accustomed to? How will I continue to pay my rent and food, car insurance, etc., if
I quit my current job? Or am I able to keep your current job and work part time at
the new business venture until it starts to generate a profit? Can I trust my partner
or employees to do an excellent job while I are gone?

IS IT FOR ME?

IS IT FOR you to have your own business, be your own boss? Are you a people person? Are you a leader? Can you be a good boss? Can you delegate duties well? Or are you comfortable with your nine-to-five and can wait go home and relax and watch some TV?

You really need to look inside yourself and decide if you have what it takes to be a boss, to run a business. This isn't for everyone, and at times, you work so many hours. It is crazy. You have to sacrifice things like going out on vacations or even spending time with your family.

RULES

EVERY BUSINESS HAS rules it must follow; some rules are enforced by the government, of the Department of Consumer Affairs, while the others are rules you will put in place for yourself and your staff to make sure everything is running professionally and smoothly.

It's always good to have a set of rules to tell us what to do, what direction to go, what protocol to follow when a situation occurs. We need additional help; we cannot just wing it. We need to follow protocol and procedures.

All employees should learn and master the rules; that way, when a client comes in, he will be treated the same no matter who helps him because all employees follow the same set of rules.

EMPLOYEES

EMPLOYEES ARE THE heart and soul of business; if you have the right staff, your day will be a lot easier, and your business will be a lot more successful. Choosing the right employees is crucial to the business because they are the ones who will be helping clients hands-on.

You need a good team so you can have a good day, and a happy boss becomes contagious. A happy boss will have your employees happy also, which in return will give you happy clients.

Employees must be trustworthy, respectful, and have great manners.

Be team players and be good around people.

If you're going to hire a family of friends, please make sure they understand the business. Business is not friendships.

Therefore, they need to listen to your demands when you request something from them; otherwise, the business will not operate at its full capacity.

CUSTOMER IS GOLD

THE CUSTOMER IS gold. Some people say that the customer is always right. That is a myth; the customer isn't always right, but it isn't a great idea to argue with a client because you might lose him. He might not return to your store, but at the same time, you cannot let a customer take advantage of you.

The customer is gold; he is the bloodline of your business. Without customers, you go out of business; therefore, you want to cater to the customer's every need. Make sure he is happy so he can feel good about spending his hard-earned cash.

If a customer walks in, first, greet him; second, listen to him—why is he in your establishment today?—third, offer him different solutions on how you can help him; last, listen to his input and feedback one more time; and finally, close the sale.

The customer will choose you over the other competition because of various reasons: you might be closer, you might have better parking outside, your prices might be cheaper, you might be faster, you might be more professional, your establishment might be cleaner, or your sales staff might be nicer.

There are many reasons why customers will choose you, but please try to distinguish yourself because of the supreme customer service you will provide not because you are cheaper. You don't want to be known as the cheapest guy on the block. Remember, if you are working really cheap, there's a possibility you will be very busy, and at the end of the week, when you count your cash, you might have no profit. Therefore, you are working just to be tired; this does not make any sense.

EQUIPMENT

YOU WANT TO buy good-quality equipment but only the equipment that you really need; don't go overboard buying equipment you don't need. Your business might grow, and you will need five printers, but to start out, you only need two, so please only buy two for now.

If you do some research, you can almost find everything used and pay half the price and save bundles of cash.

You might be able to lease the equipment and pay for it slowly so that you can save your liquidated cash for other things.

SUMMARY

I N SUMMARY, YOU want to open your own business because you are a born leader. You are tired of being bossed around. You are tired of your nine-to-five, and you know in your heart that you will be successful because everyone loves you. You just feel it in your blood that you can do a much better job than your boss can. You are ready to quit your job and open up for business. You are going to work unlimited hours until you are turning a profit. Yeah, sounds really good, but actions and reality speak louder than words. I don't want to rain on your dreams, but I want you to be prepared, and please research, research as much as you can. Add 40 percent more to your opening budget once you have calculated all expenses. Have a nice stash of at least six months of your overhead in the bank so you're not stress when you're not turning a profit.

Having your own business is great, but remember, you will become a slave to your business. You will be connected to it even when you're home at you ready for the trade off of having a business and kissing away timeless hours with your wife and kids.

When you have your own business, your life will never be the same. You will be married to that business and that lifestyle as long as that business is open. Sometimes I wonder if I would have been better off staying in my old job at the Yankee Stadium and never opening up a business. I wonder if it has been worth it or not.

I really don't have any regrets. I have a wonderful wife and three kids, but I do wish I had more time to spend with them.

Finally, if you're going into business, try not to alter your life too much, try not to borrow too much. For example, let's say you decide to refinance your house. You take out an equity loan of 40K to open up your dream business, and it doesn't work out. Two things will happen: you might lose your home because now you owe the bank and have no job to pay your mortgage, and you might also lose your marriage. A failed business might bring ruin to your marriage as well because if the business is a success, you are a genius, but it isn't, you are a failure, and now you are losing your home. Your wife will say "I want a divorce, I don't want to be near you!"

Please be careful with the choices you make, and please note, I am only sharing with you my past experiences. I am in no way a licensed professional to give you professional advice. Anything you have read in this book should not be used as a professional advice in any way or form. Please consult with the licensed lawyers and accountants for any advice you might need.

Thank you, God bless, and good luck.

www.ingramcontent.com/pod-product-compliance
Lightning Source LLC
Chambersburg PA
CBHW021933170526
45157CB00005B/2305